The Delight of the New in Cookery

No matter how old a story cooking is to us, no matter how little zest we think we have for it, we need only to have a new recipe, a new ingredient or a new method in cookery held tantalizingly before us to discover that our interest hasn't waned after all. For the quest of the new and better in cookery never loses its allure.

Even Milk has New Secrets to Reveal

Milk, perhaps more than anything else, seems to hold no novelty for us. Yet we recognize in it our most important food, supplying all the elements needed for health and growth. We know that doctors and dietitians insist upon a quart of milk a day for each member of the family. And we know that the simplest way to provide this milk is through its generous use in cooking, thereby supplying it in such a variety of form that no one tires of it.

It is therefore extremely interesting to discover that milk can contribute to our cookery a deliciousness of flavor, a smoothness of texture, a richness, a dependability of result and an economy of other materials that we have never experienced if we have confined our use of milk to ordinary bottled milk.

Only a milk of uniformly high quality and richness can produce such cooking results. To secure this uniformly high quality and richness many thousands of women have turned to a form of milk that adds immeasurably to the success of cookery—Carnation Evaporated Milk.

What Carnation Milk IS

Carnation Milk is simply the purest of rich whole milk, from fine herds, evaporated to double richness, "homogenized," and sterilized for safe keeping. To insure the quality and purity of this milk, the Carnation Company maintains at the famous Carnation Milk Farms two of the largest herds of pure bred Holsteins in the world—among them the world's greatest milk and butter producers—and introduces this high milk producing strain into the many herds of "Contented Cows" from which the milk for the Carnation condenseries is obtained. Carnation field men constantly supervise these herds to insure the proper care and feeding of the cows, and the cleanliness of the surroundings and milking methods.

It is this better milk—rushed to the Carnation condenseries in sterilized cans, tested and retested for purity and richness, evaporated to double richness, "homogenized" to break up the cream globules into minute particles and keep them uniformly distributed all through the milk, sealed in clean, air-tight cans and sterilized—that you get in every can of Carnation.

Nothing is added to it; nothing taken out except sixty per cent of the water (milk is eighty-seven per cent water as it comes from the cow). Perfect sterilization gives it a rich creamy color and insures its staying sweet and pure indefinitely.

What Carnation Milk DOES

Being doubly rich because of evaporation, Carnation Milk gives to every dish in which it is used the benefit of its double creaminess. Naturally, when you use Carnation in its concentrated form, you save decidedly on butter and cream.

Being always pure and sweet, never varying in richness and high quality Carnation gives *uniformly dependable* results in cookery. Being "homogenized," Carnation Milk with its unusually fine and evenly distributed cream particles gives a creaminess, a velvety smoothness, a fine texture, that even the finest of bottled milk cannot equal. Soups and sauces, candies and cakes, ice creams, custards, puddings, waffles and griddle cakes are among the many dishes to which Carnation gives this notably smooth, delicate texture.

Among home economics experts Carnation Milk has an extremely wide acceptance. These women, to whom cooking is both a science and an art, choose Carnation not only for the definitely improved quality which it gives to so many dishes, but because its convenient and dependable form and its freedom from waste, are in keeping with modern standards of efficiency in the kitchen.

Carnation as a Baby Food

Our best baby food, of course, is mother's milk. But if a baby can not have mother's milk, then Carnation is recommended, modified according to the physician's directions. The tiny butter fat globules, evenly distributed, make Carnation Milk easy for the baby to digest. Then too, because of the heat of sterilization, the curd formed in the stomach is softer and more easily digested than that formed by raw milk.

You can get Carnation anywhere, take it anywhere, with the utmost confidence that the milk's purity and controlled uniformity will protect the baby from upsets so often caused by milk of changing and uncertain quality. If you would like more information about Carnation for baby feeding, I will gladly send you one of our interesting folders, which deals with this subject.

Now Try Carnation

The recipes which follow have been perfected in our own kitchen, to insure your obtaining the superior results which the quality of Carnation Milk makes possible.

Order Carnation today from your grocer and prepare to enjoy "the delight of the *new* in cookery."

CARNATION MILK FOR BETTER COOKING

GENERAL DIRECTION

Making Accurate Measurements

In order to insure perfect results measurements should be accurately made and directions carefully followed. Use standard measuring cups and spoons and make all measurements absolutely level. In order to do this fill the cup or spoon and then level with a knife. Half, quarter, and third cupfuls are indicated by marks on the cup. To measure a half spoonful, fill the spoon, level, and then divide lengthwise. To measure a quarter spoonful divide the halves crosswise.

Flour should always be sifted once before measuring.

In measuring butter and other solid fats, pack solidly. When the recipe calls for a certain amount of butter melted, measure before melting. When it calls for melted butter, measure after melting.

Standard Measurements

tsp.	teaspoon
tbsp.	tablespoon
3 tsp	1 tbsp.
16 tbsp	1 cup
2 cups	1 pint
2 pints	1 quart
2 cups solid fat	1 pound
2 cups gran. sugar	1 pound
2⅔ cups powdered sugar	1 pound
2⅔ cups brown sugar	1 pound

4 cups flour   1 pound
1 sq. bitter chocolate   1 ounce

Precautions to be Observed in Heating Milk

Since milk scorches very easily it is advisable to heat it in a double boiler. If heated directly over the fire the heat should be low or an asbestos mat should be placed under the pan. If a double boiler is not used the milk requires careful watching and stirring to prevent scorching.

The Use of Carnation as Cream or Milk

If you wish to use Carnation in place of cream, use it undiluted. Used as milk, dilute it with an equal amount of water. Use half Carnation and half water in any recipe calling for milk.

Soups

Cream soups make a delightful addition to the diet and provide a splendid way to include more milk. They also are an excellent means of using left over vegetables, vegetable water, and the liquid from canned vegetables. Cream soups not only stimulate the appetite, causing the digestive juices to flow more freely, but also are very nutritious. Because Carnation Milk is rich and creamy it is the secret of the creaminess of these soups.

Garnishes for Cream Soups

What a magic effect a little garnishing has and how easily it converts a simple dish of soup into one that is deliciously attractive! The following garnishes are all suitable for cream soups:

    Vegetables cut in fancy shapes
    Dash of paprika
    Bit of chopped parsley
    Little grated cheese

Spoonful of whipped cream
Spoonful of puffed rice
Croutons
Toasted cheese sticks
Squares of custard

CREAM OF TOMATO SOUP

1 can of tomato soup
1 tall can of Carnation Milk

Heat the milk and the tomato soup in different pans but at the same time, watching carefully to prevent scorching. When both are piping hot (not boiling) and you are ready to serve, pour the hot tomato into the hot Carnation and serve immediately. To avoid curdling be sure to pour the tomato into the milk instead of vice versa. Do not combine the tomato and milk until ready to serve as these should be heated separately. This makes a thick and delicious soup. Serves 4.

CARNATION MILK MAKES CREAMY SOUPS

CREAM OF PEA SOUP

1 No. 2 can peas
1 slice onion
1½ tsp. sugar
1½ tsp. salt
⅛ tsp. pepper
2 tbsp. butter
2 tbsp. flour
1 cup Carnation Milk
1 cup water

Drain and measure liquid from peas and add enough water to make 2 cups of liquid. Add peas, onion, sugar, salt, and pepper and simmer for 15 minutes. Rub through a sieve. Make a white sauce of butter, flour, and

Carnation diluted with water. Add paprika. Combine pea mixture and white sauce and serve while hot. Serves 6.

CREAM OF POTATO SOUP

　3 medium sized potatoes
　2 slices onion
　2 tbsp. butter
　2 tbsp. flour
　1½ tsp. salt
　⅛ tsp. pepper
　¼ tsp. celery salt
　2 cups Carnation Milk
　2 cups potato water
　1 tbsp. chopped parsley

Cut potatoes in small pieces and cook with onion in boiling salted water until tender—use 3 cups of water and ½ teaspoon salt. Drain (saving the potato water) and rub the potatoes through a sieve. There should be about 2 cups of potato pulp. Make a white sauce of the butter, flour, seasonings, Carnation, and potato water. Add slowly to the potatoes, stirring to keep smooth. Reheat in the double boiler. Sprinkle with chopped parsley and serve very hot. Serves 6.

CREAM OF CELERY SOUP

　3 cups celery
　1 slice onion
　2 tbsp. butter
　3 tbsp. flour
　1 tsp. salt
　⅛ tsp. pepper
　2 cups Carnation Milk
　2 cups celery liquor
　Paprika

Wash, scrape, and cut celery in ½ inch pieces; cook with slice of onion in 3 cups boiling water until celery is soft—about 30 minutes. Drain (saving the celery liquor) and rub through a sieve. Make a white sauce of the butter, flour, seasonings, Carnation, and celery liquor. Combine celery pulp and white sauce and serve while hot. Serves 6.

CREAM OF MUSHROOM SOUP

1 can of mushrooms (8-oz.) (Get can containing stems and broken pieces)
2 tbsp. butter
3 tbsp. flour
⅛ tsp. pepper
1 tsp. salt
2 cups Carnation Milk
Paprika

Drain and measure liquor from mushrooms and add enough water to make 2 cups of liquid. Add chopped mushrooms and simmer for 15 minutes. Make white sauce of the butter, flour, seasonings, and Carnation. Add mushrooms with their liquid and serve while hot. Serves 6.

OYSTER STEW

1 pint oysters
2 cups Carnation
2 cups water
2 tbsp. butter
1 tsp. salt
⅛ tsp. pepper
¼ tsp. celery salt
1 tbsp. chopped parsley
Paprika

Carefully clean the oysters, removing any bits of shell. Heat in their own liquor until the edges curl. Season and add with butter and parsley to the 2 cups of Carnation and 2 cups of water which have been scalded together. Serves 6.

CARNATION MILK MAKES RICH SAUCES

Sauces

For Fish and Vegetables

How tempting a most ordinary food is made by the addition of an attractive sauce—one that is smooth and creamy, with delicate flavors well blended! The generous use of a variety of sauces is, to be sure, one of the secrets of French cookery. Sauces containing liberal amounts of milk not only stimulate the appetite and cause digestive juices to flow more freely but also are very nutritious.

WHITE SAUCE

	Butter	Flour
No. 1 For Cream Soups	½ tbsp.	½ tbsp.
No. 2 For Creamed Vegetables	1½ tbsp.	1½ tbsp.
No. 3 For Croquettes	3 tbsp.	3 tbsp.

½ tsp. Salt
few grains Pepper
½ cup Carnation
½ cup Water

Melt fat in top part of double boiler; add flour and seasonings and mix thoroughly. Add the Carnation diluted with the water and stir constantly until smooth and thick. Place over hot water and continue cooking for 10 minutes, stirring occasionally.

CHEESE SAUCE

Add ⅓ cup of grated cheese to 1 cup of White Sauce No. 2 and stir until it is melted. Serve hot with vegetables or fish.

PIMIENTO SAUCE

Add 3 tbsp. chopped pimiento to 1 cup of white sauce No. 2. Serve hot with vegetables or fish.

EGG SAUCE

Add 1 chopped hard cooked egg, 1 tbsp. chopped parsley, and ¼ tsp. celery salt to 1 cup of white sauce No. 2. Serve hot with vegetables or fish.

CAPER SAUCE

½ cup Carnation Milk
½ cup water
2 tbsp. butter
2 tbsp. flour
1 small onion
½ tsp. salt
⅛ tsp. pepper
¼ cup capers

Scald the Carnation and water together. Melt the butter, add chopped onion and when brown add the flour and let brown; add the salt, pepper, and scalded milk, stirring constantly. Cook for about five minutes and add the drained capers. Serve hot with fish.

MOCK HOLLANDAISE SAUCE

1 tbsp. butter
2 tbsp. flour
½ tsp. salt
⅛ tsp. pepper

¾ cup Carnation Milk
2 egg yolks
¼ cup butter
1 tbsp. lemon juice
Few grains cayenne

Follow method given above for White Sauce. Stir in beaten egg yolks after sauce is cooked and then add butter, bit by bit, and finally the lemon juice. Serve hot with vegetables or fish.

Fish

A variety of canned fish available at all times and places can be easily converted into a number of appetizing dishes which add variety to the menu. By keeping a selection of these canned products on hand the housewife is always prepared for the unexpected guest.

SALMON CROQUETTES

1 cup white sauce No. 3 (see recipe page 7)
1¾ cup flaked salmon
1 tsp. lemon juice
Salt and pepper
1 egg
Bread crumbs
Parsley

Add flaked salmon and lemon juice to white sauce and season with salt and pepper. Shape, roll in crumbs, then in slightly beaten egg, and again in the bread crumbs. Fry in deep fat, heated until hot enough to brown a piece of bread in 40 seconds (375°F). Drain and garnish with parsley. Serves 5.

SHRIMP WIGGLE

2¼ tbsp. butter
2¼ tbsp. flour
½ tsp. salt
Few grains pepper
Paprika
¾ cup Carnation Milk
¾ cup water
1 cup shrimps
1 cup canned peas

Make a white sauce of the butter, flour, seasonings, and Carnation diluted with the water. Drain the shrimps, remove the dark vein; break the shrimps into pieces and add to white sauce. Also add the drained peas. When the mixture is thoroughly heated serve on toast points. Garnish with parsley or olives. Serves 5.

TUNA FISH A LA KING

2 tbsp. butter
½ green pepper, shredded
1 hard cooked egg
½ cup chopped mushrooms
3 tbsp. flour
1 cup Carnation Milk
1 cup water
Salt and pepper
1½ cups tuna fish
½ cup peas

Sauté green pepper and mushrooms in butter until tender (about 10 minutes), keeping covered while cooking. Remove mushrooms and pepper and blend flour with the fat. Add the Carnation diluted with the water and cook until the mixture is thickened, stirring constantly to prevent lumping. Place flaked tuna fish, peas, egg, mushrooms, and pepper in top of double boiler. Pour over this the sauce and continue cooking over hot water for 10 minutes. Serve in patty shells or on toast points. Serves 6. Lobster or shrimp may be used instead of tuna fish.

Meats

Both fish and meat are important sources of tissue building material. The following recipes illustrate a few of the interesting combinations possible in preparing meat.

CREAMED CHIPPED BEEF

¼ lb. chipped beef
2 tbsp. butter
2½ tbsp. flour
Pepper
½ tsp. salt
¾ cup Carnation Milk
¾ cup water

Shred the dried beef, cover with hot water, let stand 10 minutes, then drain. Make a white sauce of the butter, flour, seasonings, and Carnation diluted with ¾ cup water. Add the chipped beef and serve on toast points or with mashed or baked potatoes. Serves 4.

CHICKEN A LA KING

2 tbsp. butter or chicken fat
¼ green pepper, shredded
¾ cup mushrooms, chopped
3 tbsp. flour
¼ pimiento, shredded
1 cup chicken broth
1 cup Carnation Milk
Salt and pepper
1½ cups cold chicken

Sauté the green pepper and mushrooms in the butter until tender (about 10 minutes), keeping them covered while cooking. Remove the mushrooms and peppers and blend the flour and seasonings with the fat left in the pan; then add the broth and Carnation and cook until thickened, stirring constantly. Place the chicken, cut in ½ inch dice, pimiento, green pepper, and mushrooms in top part of double boiler. Pour over this the sauce and continue cooking over hot water for 10 minutes. Serve in patty shells or on toast points. Serves 6.

CARNATION BAKED HAM

1 slice ham about 2 inches thick
1 tbsp. flour
2 tbsp. brown sugar
¾ cup Carnation Milk
¾ cup water

Trim off fat, cut into small pieces, and mix with the sugar. Rub the flour into the ham, then put into a baking dish. Sprinkle fat-sugar mixture over the top and pour over it the Carnation diluted with water. Place in a hot (425°F) oven. After 15 minutes reduce the temperature to 275°F—a slow oven. Bake until tender, about 2½ hours. Garnish with hard boiled eggs and parsley. Enough milk should remain for gravy. Large slice of ham serves 8.

CARNATION MILK IS CONVENIENT AND ECONOMICAL

BEEF LOAF

½ lb. pork
½ lb. veal
1 lb. beef
½ cup bread crumbs
½ onion, finely minced
⅓ cup Carnation Milk
⅓ cup water
1 egg, slightly beaten
1½ tsp. salt
Few grains pepper
4 thin slices of fat salt pork or bacon

Put meat through a food chopper, mix, and add ingredients in order given. Shape in a loaf; put in a pan and lay across the top of the loaf the slices of salt pork or bacon. Place in a hot oven (425°F). After 15 minutes reduce the heat to 300°F—a slow oven. Bake 1½ hours, basting frequently. Garnish with parsley. Serves 6.

PORK CHOPS AND POTATOES A LA CARNATION

6 potatoes
1½ tsp. salt
Few grains pepper
1 tbsp. butter
¾ cup Carnation Milk
1¼ cups water
Bread crumbs
2 tbsp. flour
6 pork chops

1 egg

Scald Carnation and water in a double boiler. Pare and slice potatoes in ¼ inch slices. Place a layer in a buttered baking dish, sprinkle with salt and pepper, dredge with flour, and dot over with bits of butter. Repeat and add the scalded milk until it can be seen through the top layer. Dip pork chops in egg and roll in bread crumbs. Place on top of potatoes and bake in a moderate (350°F) oven until the potatoes are soft. Serves 6.

CREAMED SWEET BREADS

1 lb. sweetbreads
1 tbsp. vinegar or lemon juice
⅔ cup peas
2¼ tbsp. butter
2¼ tbsp. flour
Pepper
½ tsp. salt
¾ cup Carnation
¾ cup water

Soak the sweet breads in cold water for an hour. Cook until tender (about 20 minutes) in boiling water to which ½ tsp. salt and 1 tbsp. vinegar or lemon juice have been added. When tender plunge into cold water to harden. Remove membranes and cut or break into small pieces. Add the peas. Make a white sauce of the butter, flour, seasonings, and Carnation diluted with ¾ cup water. Add sweet breads and peas, reheat and serve in patty cases or on toast points. Diced chicken or mushrooms may be added, if desired. Serves 6.

CARNATION VEAL BIRDS

1½ lbs. veal steak (¼ inch thick)
3 slices bacon
½ small onion
1 tbsp. butter

½ cup bread crumbs
½ tsp. salt
⅛ tsp. pepper
1 tsp. summer savory
3 tbsp. bacon drippings
½ cup Carnation Milk

Cut veal steak into strips 4×2½ inches, each strip making a bird. Chop trimmings of veal, bacon, and onion and brown in 1 tbsp. butter. Add bread crumbs, salt, pepper, and savory. Moisten with hot water. Spread each piece of veal with a thin layer of the mixture being careful not to put it too close to the edge. Roll and fasten with skewers or white cord. Sprinkle with salt and pepper, dredge with flour, and fry in bacon drippings until well browned. Add water to half cover the meat and cook slowly about 40 minutes or until tender. Take birds out of pan and remove skewers or cord. Add Carnation to the juice in the pan and heat. Pour this gravy over the birds and serve at once. Serves 5.

CARNATION MILK FOR CREAMING VEGETABLES

Vegetables

Serving vegetables in an attractive form is an important part of cookery because of the value of vegetables in the diet. They add the necessary bulk, some contain energy yielding material, some furnish tissue building material, but their greatest value lies in their rich mineral and vitamin content, both of which are essential for growth and for health. Doctors and dietitians advise the daily serving of at least two vegetables besides potato, one of these to be served in the raw form, as in a salad.

In order to prevent loss of minerals and destruction of vitamins it is best to cook the vegetables in the shortest time possible and in a small amount of water. Since the water in which vegetables are cooked or canned is rich in minerals it should never be discarded. It can be used for soups and for creaming the vegetables.

SPINACH AU GRATIN

3 tbsp. butter
3 tbsp. flour
½ tsp. salt
⅛ tsp. pepper
½ cup Carnation Milk
1 can Spinach (No. 2)
¾ cup Spinach liquid
¼ cup grated cheese
Stir ½ cup dried bread crumbs in 2 tbsp. butter, melted

Melt the butter; add flour and seasonings and mix thoroughly; add Carnation and the liquid drained from the can of spinach. Stir constantly until smooth and thick. Add the grated cheese and as soon as this is melted add the spinach. Put the mixture into a casserole, cover with buttered bread crumbs and put in the oven for 10 minutes or until the crumbs are browned. Serves 5.

SCALLOPED CABBAGE

   1 medium head of cabbage
   3 slices of broiled bacon
   1 cup of White Sauce No. 2 (see [page 7](page_7))
   ½ green pepper
   ½ cup bread crumbs stirred in
   2 tbsp. melted butter

Cut cabbage in quarters, cook in boiling salted water (using 1 tsp. salt to 1 quart water) until tender—about 15 minutes. Cut the broiled bacon in small squares, dice the green pepper, and add both to the white sauce. Put alternate layers of cabbage and white sauce in a casserole, shaking salt over each layer of cabbage before adding the white sauce. Cover the top layer with buttered crumbs and brown in a moderate oven. Serves 6.

CORN SOUFFLE

   3 tbsp. butter
   4 tbsp. flour
   1 tsp. salt
   ⅛ tsp. pepper
   ¼ tsp. celery salt
   ½ cup Carnation Milk
   ½ cup water
   1 cup canned corn
   2 tbsp. chopped pimiento
   3 eggs

Make white sauce of the butter, flour, seasonings, and Carnation diluted with the water. Add the corn, pimiento, and beaten egg yolks. Fold in beaten egg whites and pour into buttered baking dish; bake in a slow oven until firm (about 30 minutes). Serves 5.

CREAMED VEGETABLES

Use 2 cups of vegetable to one cup of white sauce No. 2 (see page 7). In making the white sauce use the water in which the vegetables have been cooked, rather than plain water. Pour the white sauce over the vegetables and mix gently with a fork so as to preserve the dices, squares, strips, or slices of vegetable. Variety may be obtained by adding grated cheese, diced pimiento, shredded green pepper, chips of broiled bacon, or celery salt to the white sauce.

STUFFED BAKED POTATO

6 medium sized potatoes
2 tbsp. butter
1 tsp. salt
½ tsp. pepper
2 tbsp. Carnation Milk
2 tbsp. water
1 egg white
2 tbsp. grated cheese

Bake potatoes in a hot oven for 45 minutes or until soft. Remove from oven and cut off the top third of each; then scoop out insides. Mash potatoes, add seasoning, and then the Carnation and water heated together; beat well; add egg white well beaten. Refill potato shell; sprinkle top with grated cheese and put into a hot oven to brown. Serve at once. Serves 6.

BAKED CAULIFLOWER

1 medium cauliflower
1 cup white sauce No. 2 (see recipe page 7)
⅓ cup bread crumbs stirred in
1 tbsp. melted butter

Remove leaves and trim off stalk from the cauliflower. Soak in a solution of 1 tbsp. vinegar, 1 tsp. salt, and 1 quart of cold water for 5 minutes to remove dirt and insects. Cook whole, stem up, in boiling salted water until tender (about 10 minutes). Put cauliflower in a buttered baking dish, pour the white sauce over it, and cover with buttered bread crumbs. Brown in a moderate oven. Serves 6.

Salads

Salads served crisp and cold add zest and variety to any meal. The secret of an attractive salad is to have all of the ingredients thoroughly chilled and drained. In combining them use a fork, mixing carefully so as not to mash the ingredients. Add the dressing just before serving.

TOMATO SALAD

    6 tomatoes
    1 head of lettuce
    Mayonnaise

Select tomatoes of good shape and color. Peel and cut 3 thin slices off the top of each tomato and arrange on lettuce on salad plates. Cover slices and top of tomato with mayonnaise (see page 14); sprinkle with paprika.

If desired, the inside of the tomato may be scooped out and the cup sprinkled with salt. Then invert and chill; when ready to serve add a chicken filling made by combining 1 cup chopped chicken, ½ cup diced celery, and ⅓ cup nuts with mayonnaise. Or a vegetable filling may be made by combining diced tomato, ¾ cup of diced celery, ⅓ cup nuts, and ½ cup chopped olives or sweet pickles with mayonnaise. Serves 6.

STUFFED CELERY

6 stalks celery
⅔ cup cream cheese
2 tbsp. Carnation Milk
¼ tsp. salt
1 tsp. onion juice
Paprika
Mayonnaise
1 tsp. chopped green pepper
Lettuce leaves

Select crisp stalks of celery having deep grooves. Add milk and seasoning to the cream cheese. Pile mixture securely into the grooves of celery, leaving a fluffy, rough surface. Cut into 4 inch lengths. Select a small crisp celery tip and place into one end. Sprinkle with paprika and lay two or three stalks on a lettuce leaf. Serve with mayonnaise (see page 14). Serves 6.

CARNATION MAKES THE DRESSING CREAMY

PEACH SALAD

6 peaches
Lemon juice
2 tbsp. Carnation Milk
½ cup cream cheese
Lettuce leaves
½ cup mayonnaise

Peel and cut peaches in half (or use halves of canned peaches). Sprinkle with lemon juice to prevent discoloring. Place 2 halves on lettuce leaf on each salad plate. Soften cheese with the Carnation Milk and combine with the mayonnaise. Put mixture into a pastry bag and fill the hollows of peaches leaving a rose on top, or simply fill carefully with a spoon. Serves 6.

CARNATIONNAISE
(Mayonnaise)

4 tbsp. flour
1 tbsp. sugar
1 tbsp. mustard
1 tsp. salt
Paprika
1 cup salad oil
⅔ cup Carnation Milk
¼ cup cider vinegar
¾ cup water
1 egg

Mix dry ingredients and to this add gradually ¼ cup of salad oil, ¼ cup of cider vinegar, and ¾ cup of water. Stir until smooth. Cook over a slow fire until thick and the flour is well cooked, stirring constantly. Remove from fire and beat into the mixture 1 egg (which has been slightly beaten), ⅔ cup of Carnation Milk, and ¾ cup of salad oil. Add the milk and oil slowly and beat very smooth. This makes 3 cups of mayonnaise. It will keep indefinitely.

FRUIT SALAD DRESSING

Carnationnaise is delicious for fruit salads. If a creamier dressing is desired combine ½ cup whipped Carnation (see directions page 31) and 1 cup of Carnationnaise.

THOUSAND ISLAND DRESSING

2 cups Carnationnaise
½ cup Chili sauce
1 tsp. finely cut onion
3 tbsp. diced pimiento
3 tbsp. diced green pepper
2 hard cooked eggs, cut fine
3 tbsp. chopped sweet pickle

Mix the ingredients and keep in a cool place until ready to use. Excellent with any vegetable salad.

NO EGG MAYONNAISE

½ tsp. salt
Few grains pepper
½ tsp. mustard
½ tsp. sugar
¼ tsp. paprika
2 tbsp. Carnation Milk
½ cup salad oil
1 tbsp. lemon juice or vinegar

Mix dry ingredients with Carnation. Add oil gradually, beating constantly. Add lemon juice or vinegar and beat until smooth. This makes ⅔ cup of dressing.

COOKED SALAD DRESSING

1 tsp. mustard
1 tsp. salt
Dash cayenne
2 tbsp. sugar
1½ tbsp. flour
½ cup Carnation Milk
2 egg yolks, beaten
½ cup water

2 tbsp. melted butter
¼ cup vinegar

Mix dry ingredients in top of double boiler. Gradually add egg yolks and butter; then add the Carnation diluted with the water; stir constantly to keep smooth. Cook over hot water for 10 minutes. Remove from fire, cool, and add vinegar.

CARNATION MILK FOR BETTER BAKING

Quick Breads

Breads which are lightened by means of yeast (see recipe [page 30](page_30)) are called "yeast breads" while those lightened by other leavening agents are termed "quick breads". The latter can be prepared in a very short time and are intended to be served at once while they are fresh and hot.

PLAIN MUFFINS

   2 cups bread flour
   4 tsp. baking powder
   2 tbsp. sugar
   ¾ tsp. salt
   1 egg
   ⅓ cup Carnation Milk
   ⅔ cup water
   2 tbsp. melted fat

Sift dry ingredients. Beat egg and add Carnation diluted with the water; add melted fat. Stir liquid quickly into the dry ingredients. Pour immediately into oiled muffin tins. Bake 20-25 minutes in a hot (425°F) oven. Makes 12 muffins.

GRAHAM DATE MUFFINS

   1 cup bread flour
   1 cup graham flour
   4 tsp. baking powder
   2 tbsp. sugar
   ¾ tsp. salt
   ½ cup chopped dates
   2 tbsp. melted fat

1 egg
⅓ cup Carnation Milk
⅔ cup water

Sift the bread flour, baking powder, sugar, and salt and add to the graham flour; add the dates. Beat the egg and add Carnation diluted with the water; add melted fat. Stir liquids quickly into the dry ingredients. Pour immediately into oiled muffin tins. Bake 20-25 minutes in a hot oven (425°F). Makes 12 muffins.

NUT BREAD

1½ cups bread flour
1½ cups graham flour
4 tsp. baking powder
⅓ cup sugar
1 tsp. salt
1 egg
1 cup chopped nuts
¾ cup water
¾ cup Carnation Milk
2 tbsp. fat, melted

Sift baking powder, sugar, salt, and bread flour and add to the graham flour; add the chopped nuts. Mix the melted fat, Carnation diluted with the water, and well beaten egg. Combine liquids quickly with the dry ingredients. Pour into a greased loaf pan, cover and let stand for 20 minutes; bake in a hot (400°F) oven.

JIFFY COFFEE CAKE

2 cups flour
3 tsp. baking powder
¼ cup sugar
½ cup cold fat
½ cup currants
⅓ cup Carnation Milk
⅔ cup water
1 egg

Sift the dry ingredients, rub or cut in the fat, and add the currants. Mix the beaten egg with the Carnation diluted with the water; add to the flour mixture. Pour into a greased pan, sprinkle with sugar and cinnamon, and bake in a moderate (375°F) oven for about 40 minutes.

The same recipe may be used for a DUTCH APPLE CAKE. After the mixture is poured into the pan, press sharp edge of sliced apples into dough in parallel rows. Sprinkle top with 3 tbsp. sugar mixed with ½ tsp. cinnamon. Bake in a moderate (375°F) oven for 40 minutes.

BAKING POWDER BISCUITS

2 cups bread flour
4 tsp. baking powder
1 tsp. salt
4 tbsp. cold fat
2 tsp. sugar
¼ cup Carnation Milk
½ cup water

Sift dry ingredients, rub in shortening with finger tips or cut in with two knives. Add Carnation diluted with the water and mix to soft dough. Toss on slightly floured board, roll or pat out to ¾ inch thickness, and cut with biscuit cutter. Brush top with thin layer of melted fat. Bake in a hot (450°F) oven for 10 to 12 minutes. Makes about 14 biscuits. EMERGENCY BISCUITS are made by using the same recipe, changing the liquid to ⅓ cup Carnation and ⅔ cup water. Drop by spoonsful onto a greased tin and bake.

PIN WHEEL BISCUITS

2 cups bread flour
4 tsp. baking powder
1 tsp. salt
3 tbsp. sugar
4 tbsp. cold fat
¼ cup Carnation Milk
½ cup water
⅓ cup chopped raisins
2 tbsp. chopped citron
⅓ tsp. cinnamon
2 tbsp. sugar

Sift the first four ingredients, rub or cut in the shortening. Add Carnation diluted with the water and mix to soft dough. Toss on slightly floured board, pat or roll to ¼ inch thickness, sprinkle with raisins, citron, cinnamon, and sugar. Roll like a jelly roll. Cut off pieces ¾ inch in thickness and place on a greased tin. Bake in a hot oven (450°F) for 10 to 15 minutes.

SCONES

2 cups pastry flour
4 tsp. baking powder
2 tsp. sugar
1 tsp. salt
4 tbsp. fat
2 eggs
3 tbsp. Carnation Milk
3 tbsp. water

Sift dry ingredients, rub or cut in fat. Dilute Carnation with water; add milk with beaten eggs (reserving a little of the egg white); mix to soft dough. Roll out to ¾ inch thickness, cut into squares or diamond shapes. Brush over with a little of the reserved egg white and sprinkle with sugar. Bake in a hot (450°F) oven.

Cakes

The secret of making a light, feathery cake of velvety smoothness lies in the selection of materials of good quality, accurate measurements, and correct blending of ingredients. Always sift the flour once before measuring. Carefully follow the directions given for combining ingredients. To obtain a level cake it is well to push the dough toward the corners of the pan before putting the cake in the oven. When the cake is well browned, shrunken from the edge of the pan, and when the dough springs back quickly if slightly dented in the center, the cake is done.

DEVIL'S FOOD CAKE

1¾ cups pastry flour
2 tsp. baking powder
½ tsp. soda
½ tsp. salt
5 tbsp. Carnation Milk
5 tbsp. water

1 cup sugar
⅜ cup fat
2 eggs
2 squares chocolate
½ tsp. vanilla

Measure flour after sifting once. Resift with baking powder, soda, and salt. Dilute the Carnation Milk with the water. Cream fat and sugar thoroughly. Add well beaten eggs and beat until mixture is light colored and fluffy. Add the melted chocolate and stir until well blended. Add flour and milk alternately to the creamed mixture, beginning and ending with the flour as this helps to keep the mixture creamy. Add vanilla the last few stirs. Pour immediately into pan that has been well oiled and dusted with a thin film of flour. Bake in a moderate (360°F) oven.

PLAIN CAKE

1⅓ cups pastry flour
2½ tsp. baking powder
¼ tsp. salt
3 tbsp. Carnation Milk
5 tbsp. water
¼ cup fat
¾ cup sugar
1 egg
½ tsp. vanilla

Measure flour after it has been sifted once. Resift flour with baking powder and salt. Dilute the Carnation with the water. Cream the fat and sugar thoroughly. Add well beaten egg and beat until the mixture is a light color and creamy. Add the flour and milk alternately to the creamed mixture, beginning and ending with the flour, as this helps to keep the mixture creamy. Add the flavoring last. Pour into tins that have been oiled and dusted with a thin film of flour. Bake in a moderate (375°F) oven.

CARNATION MAKES FINE TEXTURE CAKES

SPICE CAKE

1 tsp. cinnamon
½ tsp. nutmeg
½ tsp. cloves
Few grains cayenne
1½ tbsp. boiling water
1¾ cups pastry flour
3 tsp. baking powder
¼ tsp. salt
2 eggs
4 tbsp. Carnation Milk
6 tbsp. water
½ cup fat
1 cup sugar

Soak spices in boiling water. Measure flour after sifting once. Resift twice with the baking powder and salt. Dilute Carnation with the water. Cream fat and sugar thoroughly. Add well beaten eggs and beat until the mixture is light and fluffy. Add spices, then the flour and milk alternately, beginning and ending with the flour. Bake in a moderate (375°F) oven.

WHITE CAKE

1½ cups pastry flour
3 tsp. baking powder
½ tsp. salt
2 tbsp. Carnation Milk
½ tsp. vanilla or almond
6 tbsp. water
⅜ cup fat
1 cup sugar
2 egg whites

Measure flour after sifting once. Resift with baking powder and salt. Dilute Carnation with the water. Cream fat and sugar thoroughly. Add unbeaten egg whites and beat until mixture is very light. Add flour and milk alternately, beginning and ending with flour. Add flavoring. Bake in a moderate (375°F) oven.

CARAMEL NUT CAKE

1½ cups pastry flour
2 tsp. baking powder
¼ tsp. salt
¼ cup Carnation Milk
¼ cup water
⅓ cup shortening
1 cup brown sugar
2 eggs
½ cup chopped nuts
½ tsp. vanilla

Measure flour after sifting once. Resift with baking powder and salt. Dilute Carnation with the water. Cream fat and sugar thoroughly. Add well beaten eggs and beat until mixture is light and creamy. Dredge the nuts with part of the flour. Add flour and milk alternately to the creamed mixture, beginning and ending with the flour. Add the nuts and vanilla. Bake in a moderate (375°F) oven. Ice with Caramel Icing (Page 26).

LEMON COCOANUT COOKIES

1½ cups pastry flour
2 tsp. baking powder
Few grains salt
2 tbsp. Carnation Milk
3 tbsp. water
¼ cup fat
1 cup cocoanut
½ cup sugar
1 egg
½ tsp. lemon extract

Mix as for Plain Cake (page 17). Add flavoring and cocoanut at the last. Drop by spoonful on oiled tins, allowing about 2 inches space between each cooky. Bake in a hot (400°F) oven.

FUDGE SQUARES

1 cup pastry flour
1 tsp. baking powder
Few grains salt
2 tbsp. Carnation Milk
2 tbsp. water
¼ cup fat
1 cup sugar
2 eggs
2 squares chocolate
1 tsp. vanilla
⅓ cup nuts

Mix as for Devil's Food Cake (page 17). Pour ½ inch deep into a cake pan that has been well oiled and dusted with a thin film of flour. Bake in a moderate (375°F) oven. Ice with Fudge Icing (page 26). Cut in squares.

CARNATION IS PURE MILK, DOUBLE RICH

Pastry

Home made pies "like mother used to make"! Doesn't that anticipation make your mouth water? And really, pastry making is not such a difficult culinary task if the following precautions are observed.

Keep all ingredients as cold as possible. If the fat is rubbed into the flour with the fingers, use quick and light motion for if the fat is melted the crust will be tough. Use the minimum amount of water needed to hold the dough together. Chilling the dough before rolling makes it easier to handle and also lighter. Roll just enough dough for one crust at a time. Use quick light motion, from the center outward so as to keep the shape round.

Do not grease the pie tin. Fit dough smoothly to pie tin so no air is enclosed. If crust is to be baked before the filling is added, the pie tin may be inverted and the dough fitted on the outside. Handle dough as little as possible. Bake in hot oven (450°F).

PLAIN PASTRY

2 cups pastry flour or 1¾ cups bread flour
½ cup cold fat
1 tsp. salt
Approximately ⅓ cup cold water

Sift flour and salt; cut or rub in shortening; add the cold water gradually, adding just enough to hold the dough together. Let chill for 20 minutes. Divide dough in two parts and roll out to ⅛ inch thickness on a slightly floured board. Line pie tin, crimp edge with thumb and finger; prick sides and bottom with fork to preserve the shape. Bake in a hot oven (450°F) for 12 to 20 minutes. For a two crust pie, line the pie tin with pastry, moisten rim with cold water, add filling and cover with top crust which has incisions cut in it to allow the escape of steam. Press edges of upper and lower dough together, trim off excess and bake in a hot oven (450°F). This recipe makes 2 crusts.

PUMPKIN PIE

   1¼ cups steamed pumpkin
   ⅞ cup brown sugar
   1 tsp. cinnamon
   1 tsp. ginger
   2 tbsp. orange juice
   ½ tsp. salt
   2 eggs
   1 cup Carnation Milk
   ¼ cup water

Mix materials in order given and pour into an unbaked pastry shell. Place in a hot (450°F) oven to set the crust. After 10 minutes reduce the temperature to 250°F for the rest of the period. Bake about 1 hour. Makes 1 pie.

BUTTERSCOTCH PIE

   1½ cups brown sugar
   ½ cup flour
   ½ tsp. salt
   1¾ cups Carnation Milk
   ⅞ cup water
   3 tbsp. butter
   3 eggs

Mix sugar, flour, and salt thoroughly; scald Carnation and water together; add milk to dry mixture stirring until well blended. Return to the double boiler and cook for 25 minutes, stirring occasionally; add to well beaten egg yolks and continue cooking for 2 minutes; add butter. Pour filling into baked pastry shell. Cover with meringue made by folding 4 tbsp. sugar and ¼ tsp. baking powder into 3 stiffly beaten egg whites. Brown in a slow oven

(300°F). Makes 1 large pie. To make RAISIN BUTTERSCOTCH PIE use the same recipe, adding 1 cup of raisins to the filling.

LEMON CREAM PIE

1½ cups sugar
4½ tbsp. flour
Few grains salt
¾ cup Carnation Milk
1 tsp. grated lemon rind
5 tbsp. lemon juice
1 tbsp. butter
2 eggs
¾ cup water

Mix sugar, flour, and salt thoroughly; scald Carnation with the water; add milk to dry mixture, stirring until well blended. Return to the double boiler and cook for 25 minutes, stirring occasionally; add to well beaten egg yolks and continue cooking for 2 minutes; add butter, lemon juice and rind. Pour filling into baked pastry shell. Cover with meringue made by folding 2 tbsp. powdered sugar or granulated sugar and ⅛ tsp. baking powder into 2 stiffly beaten egg whites. Brown in a slow (300°F) oven. Makes 1 pie.

PINEAPPLE PIE

    4 tbsp. flour
    ⅔ cup sugar
    ⅛ tsp. salt
    1⅓ cups crushed pineapple
    1 cup Carnation Milk
    1 cup water
    ⅔ tsp. vanilla
    3 eggs

Follow method given for lemon pie, adding vanilla and well drained pineapple in place of the lemon. Use 4 tbsp. sugar, ¼ tsp. baking powder and 3 egg whites for the meringue. Makes 1 large pie.

CHOCOLATE PIE

    2 squares chocolate
    1 cup boiling water
    1 cup Carnation Milk
    4 tbsp. flour
    ⅞ cup sugar
    ¼ tsp. salt
    3 eggs
    1 tbsp. butter
    ½ tsp. vanilla

Melt the chocolate, add the boiling water and milk and continue heating until the mixture is smooth. Mix flour, sugar, and salt and add the hot chocolate mixture gradually, stirring so as to prevent lumping. Return to double boiler and cook 25 minutes, stirring occasionally. Pour over the well beaten egg yolks beating constantly. Return to double boiler and cook 2 minutes longer. Add flavoring and pour into baked pastry shell. Cover with meringue made by folding 4 tbsp. sugar and ¼ tsp. baking powder into stiffly beaten egg whites. Brown in a slow (300°F) oven. Makes 1 pie.

Puddings

The desserts presented here are suggested as a means of including more milk in the diet, in order that the advised quota (1 quart daily for each member of the family) may be included. Consider the dessert in its relation to the whole meal so that it will supply dietary needs which have not been filled in the other courses. Serve a light dessert with heavy meals, and heavy desserts with light meals.

CHOCOLATE BLANC MANGE

2 tbsp. cornstarch
⅓ cup sugar
¼ tsp. salt
1⅓ cups cold water
1 cup Carnation Milk
1½ squares unsweetened chocolate
1 egg
1 tsp. vanilla

Combine cornstarch, sugar, and salt, mixing thoroughly. Mix with ⅓ cup cold water and add slowly to 1 cup of Carnation which has been diluted and scalded with 1 cup of water. Cook over hot water for 15 minutes, stirring constantly until thickened. Melt chocolate and add to cooked mixture; then add to the well beaten egg and cook 2 minutes longer. Remove from fire, add flavoring and chill. Serves 5.

COCOANUT BLANC MANGE

¼ cup cornstarch
¼ cup sugar
½ tsp. salt
1 cup water
1 cup Carnation Milk
⅔ cup cocoanut
2 egg whites
½ tsp. vanilla

Mix cornstarch, sugar, and salt with ½ cup cold water. Dilute Carnation with ½ cup water and scald; add the cornstarch mixture slowly to the scalded milk. Cook in a double boiler for 20 minutes, stirring constantly until thickened. Cool slightly and add the shredded cocoanut, stiffly beaten egg whites and the vanilla. Nuts, dates, or candied cherries may be added if desired. Serves 5.

CARNATION MAKES TASTY PUDDINGS

CHOCOLATE BREAD PUDDING

2 squares bitter chocolate
¾ cup sugar
2 cups Carnation Milk
2 cups hot water
2 cups stale bread crumbs
2 eggs
¼ tsp. salt

1 tsp. vanilla

Melt the chocolate; add the sugar and 1 cup of Carnation diluted with 1 cup of water; cook until the mixture is smooth. Soak crumbs for 20 minutes in 1 cup of Carnation diluted with 1 cup of water; then combine with chocolate mixture. Add slightly beaten eggs, salt, and flavoring. Pour into a greased baking dish, set in a pan of hot water, and bake in a slow (300°F) oven for 1 hour. Serves 8.

LEMON RICE CREAM

½ cup rice
½ cup sugar
½ tsp. salt
1½ cups Carnation Milk
1½ cups water
Grated rind of ¾ lemon
2 tbsp. powdered sugar
2½ tbsp. lemon juice
2 eggs
¼ tsp. lemon extract

Wash rice and soak in cold water for an hour. Drain, put into double boiler; add the Carnation diluted with 1½ cups water; add salt and cook until rice is soft. Add sugar, lemon rind, lemon juice, and egg yolks slightly beaten. Cook until it thickens, about 5 minutes, then turn into a buttered baking dish, cover with a meringue made from egg whites, powdered sugar, and lemon extract. Put in a slow (300°F) oven just long enough to brown. Serves 8.

PINEAPPLE RICE PUDDING

½ cup rice
½ cup sugar
1½ cups Carnation Milk
1½ cups water

1 cup crushed pineapple
2 eggs
½ tsp. salt

Wash rice and soak in cold water for an hour. Drain; put into double boiler; add Carnation diluted with 1½ cups water; add salt and cook until rice is soft. Add sugar, egg yolks slightly beaten, and grated pineapple. Fold in the stiffly beaten egg whites, pour into a buttered baking dish and bake for about 30 minutes in a slow (300°F) oven.

DATE TAPIOCA CREAM

⅓ cup tapioca
Few grains salt
1 cup sugar
2 cups Carnation Milk
2 cups water
2 small eggs
1 cup chopped dates
1 tsp. vanilla

Heat the Carnation and water together. Add tapioca, salt, and sugar to hot milk. Cook in a double boiler for 25 minutes, or until tapioca is transparent. Pour into well beaten eggs, return to double boiler and continue cooking for 2 minutes. Add vanilla and dates. Chill. Serves 8.

CARAMEL TAPIOCA

⅓ cup tapioca
Few grains salt
2 small eggs
2 cups Carnation Milk
2 cups water
1 cup light brown sugar
½ cup nut meats
1 tsp. vanilla

Heat the Carnation and water together. Add tapioca, salt, and sugar to hot milk. Cook in a double boiler for 25 minutes, or until tapioca is transparent. Pour into well beaten eggs, return to double boiler and continue cooking for 2 minutes longer. Add vanilla and nuts. Chill. Serves 8.

CARNATION MAKES DELICIOUS DESSERTS

Gelatine Desserts

In making the following desserts be sure to chill the Carnation Milk thoroughly before whipping.

CHOCOLATE CHARLOTTE

1⅛ tbsp. gelatine
2 tbsp. cold water
½ cup sugar
1½ cups Carnation Milk
½ cup water
1 square bitter chocolate
½ tsp. vanilla
½ doz. lady fingers

Soak granulated gelatine in 2 tbsp. cold water for 5 minutes. Melt shaved chocolate in double boiler, add sugar, ½ cup water, and ½ cup Carnation. Let cook 5 minutes or until smooth; pour over gelatine and stir until dissolved. When cool, add the vanilla. Whip 1 cup of Carnation which has been chilled for a couple of hours, gradually add the chocolate and gelatine mixture and stir until it begins to thicken. When well thickened pour carefully into a mold which has been lined with lady fingers. Let stand in a cold place for an hour or more. When ready to serve turn out on a flat dish, cover with whipped cream, and garnish with maraschino cherries or nuts. Serves 5.

MACAROON DESSERT

1¼ tbsp. gelatine
¾ cup water
9 macaroons, crumbled

1¾ cup Carnation Milk
2 egg yolks, slightly beaten
¼ cup sugar
1 tsp. vanilla

Soak gelatine for 5 minutes in ¼ cup water mixed with ¼ cup of Carnation. Scald ½ cup of Carnation diluted with ½ cup of water; pour over slightly beaten egg yolks to which the sugar has been added; cook in a double boiler until the mixture thickens slightly (about 3 minutes); pour over the gelatine and stir until dissolved. When cool, add the vanilla. Whip 1 cup of Carnation which has been chilled for a couple of hours, gradually add the gelatine mixture and stir until it begins to thicken. Add the crumbled macaroons and pour into a mold. Let stand in a cold place for an hour or more. When ready to serve turn out on a flat dish and garnish as desired. Serves 5.

PINEAPPLE BAVARIAN CREAM

1¼ tbsp. gelatine
¼ cup cold water
1 cup Carnation Milk
1 cup grated pineapple and juice
⅛ tsp. salt
3 tbsp. lemon juice
½ cup sugar

Soak gelatine in cold water for 5 minutes. Heat pineapple, sugar and salt; add the soaked gelatine and lemon juice. Set in a pan of cold water to cool. Whip the Carnation which has been chilled for a couple of hours; as soon as the pineapple mixture begins to thicken add it to the whipped Carnation. Pour into a mold and chill. Serves 5.

PRUNE CREAM

1 cup chopped cooked prunes
1½ tbsp. lemon juice

¼ cup powdered sugar
¾ cup Carnation Milk
¼ tsp. gelatine

Whip Carnation Milk, following directions on page 31. Add lemon juice, sugar, and few grains of salt to chopped cooked prunes. Fold the prune mixture into the whipped Carnation. Serves 5.

Ice Creams

Ice Cream is not only a delightful and refreshing dessert but also a valuable food. Because Carnation Milk is double rich it makes an especially delicious ice cream.

PINEAPPLE ICE CREAM

  4 cups Carnation Milk
  ½ tbsp. gelatine
  1 cup of sugar
  1 cup grated pineapple

Heat one cup of Carnation; soak the gelatine in 1 tbsp. cold milk, and add to the hot milk; stir until dissolved. Strain the pineapple, using only the dry grated fruit. Add the remaining milk, pineapple, and sugar, to the gelatine mixture. Stir until everything is well blended. Chill and freeze, using 1 part of salt to 5 parts of ice. Serves 10.

CHOCOLATE ICE CREAM

1 cup sugar
Few grains salt
4 cups of Carnation Milk
2 sqs. of bitter chocolate
3 eggs
1 tsp. vanilla

Heat the milk with the sugar in the double boiler. Melt the chocolate and add to the hot milk; continue heating until mixture is well blended. Pour into the well beaten eggs; return to double boiler and continue cooking for 2 minutes. Add salt and flavoring. Chill and freeze, using 1 part of salt to 5 parts of ice. Serves 10.

BANANA ICE CREAM

5 good sized bananas
4 cups Carnation Milk
1 cup sugar
2 tbsp. lemon juice

Crush bananas to a soft pulp. Add Carnation, sugar, and lemon juice. Stir until sugar is thoroughly dissolved. Chill and freeze, using 1 part of salt to 5 parts of ice. Serves 10.

ORANGE SHERBERT

1 lemon
1 orange
½ cup sugar
2 cups Carnation Milk
2 egg whites

Grate rinds of lemon and orange, squeeze out juice. Add grated rind and sugar to Carnation; then add gradually the lemon and orange juice, stirring constantly. The milk may have a slightly curdled appearance after this but it disappears in the freezing. Freeze partially, then add the egg whites beaten stiff, and continue freezing. Serves 5.

Miscellaneous Desserts

STRAWBERRY SHORTCAKE

2 cups bread flour
4 tsp. baking powder
1 tsp. salt
5 tbsp. fat
1 tbsp. sugar
¼ cup Carnation Milk
½ cup cold water

Sift dry ingredients, rub in fat, add Carnation diluted with water, and mix quickly. Toss on slightly floured board, pat to 1 inch thickness, and put in layer cake tins. Cover top with thin layer of melted fat. Cover and let stand for 10 minutes. Bake about 12 minutes in hot (450°F) oven. Put sweetened and slightly crushed berries between and on top of shortcake. Save a few large berries to put on top.

CHEESE TORTE

1 package of zwieback (6 oz.)
2 cups of sugar
1 tsp. cinnamon
1½ lb. cottage cheese
⅓ cup butter, melted
4 eggs
½ cup chopped nuts
Few grains salt
4 tbsp. flour
Juice and rind of ½ lemon
½ tsp. vanilla
1 cup Carnation Milk

Roll zwieback fine; mix with 1 cup sugar, cinnamon, and melted butter. Line a buttered spring cake pan or other baking dish with this mixture, saving ⅔ cup for the top. Press the mixture on the bottom and sides of the baking dish. Beat eggs well and add 1 cup of sugar, salt, flavoring, Carnation, cheese, and flour. Mix all together and press the mixture through a sieve. Beat well, add nuts and pour into the lined mold. Put crumbs on top and bake in a moderate oven (325°F) for 1 hour. Turn off heat and let stand in oven 1 hour or until cool. Serves 10.

CUP CUSTARD

2 cups Carnation Milk
2 cups water
5 eggs
½ cup sugar
½ tsp. salt
1 tsp. vanilla

Scald Carnation and water; beat eggs slightly, add sugar, salt, vanilla and scalded milk. Pour into individual buttered custard cups, set in a pan of hot water. Sprinkle with nutmeg, and bake in a slow (225°F) oven until a knife inserted in the center comes out clean. Requires about 40 minutes. Serves 8.

Dessert Sauces and Cake Icings

The following delicious sauces and icings will give even the simplest pudding and cake a most festive air.

BUTTERSCOTCH SAUCE

⅔ cup light corn syrup
1 cup light brown sugar
¾ cup Carnation Milk
Chopped nuts, if desired
4 tbsp. butter

Cook sugar, syrup, and butter to form a thick syrup (the soft ball stage, 235°F). Remove from the fire; beat in the Carnation and nuts. Keep warm over water. May be served on pudding, cake, or ice cream.

FUDGE SAUCE

1 tbsp. butter
2 squares chocolate
2 tbsp. corn syrup
½ cup Carnation Milk
1 tsp. vanilla
⅓ cup water
2 cups sugar

Melt butter and shaved chocolate; add sugar, syrup, and Carnation diluted with the water; cook until mixture forms a very soft ball in cold water. Add vanilla and beat slightly. Keep warm over water. May be served on pudding, cake, or ice cream.

CARAMEL ICING

    2 cups light brown sugar
    ⅓ cup Carnation Milk
    ⅓ cup water
    1 tbsp. butter
    ½ tsp. vanilla

Mix sugar and Carnation diluted with the water; cook until it forms a soft ball in cold water. Add the butter, cool, add vanilla, and beat until creamy. Spread on the cake.

FUDGE ICING

    1 tbsp. butter
    2 squares chocolate
    2 cups sugar
    ⅓ cup Carnation Milk
    ⅓ cup water
    ½ tsp. vanilla
    1 tbsp. corn syrup

Melt butter and shaved chocolate; add sugar, corn syrup, and Carnation diluted with water. Cook until mixture forms a soft ball in cold water. Cool, add vanilla, and beat until creamy. Spread on the cake.

UNCOOKED CHOCOLATE ICING

    2 tbsp. chocolate
    2 tbsp. Carnation Milk
    ½ tsp. vanilla
    1 cup powdered sugar

Melt chocolate, add Carnation, vanilla, and sugar and mix thoroughly. Spread on the cake.

OPERA ICING

2 cups powdered sugar
½ cup Carnation Milk
2 tbsp. butter

Mix ingredients and heat slowly to dissolve sugar. Boil 2 minutes. When a little of the mixture is dropped into cold water, it should just hold together. Remove from fire, beat until creamy and spread.

CARNATION MILK FOR CREAMY CANDIES

Candies

The candy maker who aspires to make smooth, creamy candy may be interested in trying the following suggestions:

Use Carnation Milk because it is so rich and creamy. Carnation makes especially delicious candy because of its homogenization. In this process the butter fat particles are finely divided and evenly distributed. For this reason Carnation blends thoroughly with the other ingredients and makes an unusually smooth and creamy candy.

Use corn syrup or cream of tartar as these help to keep the candy from becoming grainy.

While the candy is cooking stir just enough to prevent scorching. Too much stirring is liable to make the candy grainy.

After the candy is cooked let it stand until it is almost cold. Then beat vigorously until it is thick and creamy.

CARNATION FUDGE

2 tbsp. butter
2 sq. chocolate
3 cups sugar
2 tbsp. corn syrup (light)
½ cup Carnation Milk
½ cup water
1 tsp. vanilla
Chopped nuts, if desired.

Melt butter and shaved chocolate in a sauce pan; add sugar, corn syrup, and Carnation diluted with the water. Cook until mixture forms a soft ball in cold water or reaches a temperature of 235°F, stirring occasionally to prevent sticking. Remove from fire and let stand until cool. When cool add vanilla and beat until creamy; add chopped nuts and mold on a buttered plate. FUDGE BALLS may be made by forming the candy into balls and rolling in chopped nuts, cocoanut, grated chocolate, or dipping in melted chocolate. MARSHMALLOW FUDGE may be made by adding 1 cup of cut marshmallows instead of the nuts.

PEANUT BUTTER FUDGE

2 cups sugar
2 tbsp. corn syrup
⅓ cup Carnation Milk
⅓ cup water
2 tbsp. peanut butter
½ tsp. vanilla
½ cup chopped peanuts, if desired.

Cook sugar, corn syrup, and Carnation diluted with the water. When it reaches the soft ball stage, remove from fire and add peanut butter. When cool add vanilla and beat until creamy. Mold on a buttered plate.

CREAM CARAMELS

2 cups sugar
2 cups corn syrup
½ cup butter
¼ tsp. salt
2 cups Carnation Milk
1 tsp. vanilla

Cook sugar, syrup, salt, and butter until the mixture reaches a clear, thick consistency. Stir in gradually the Carnation Milk. Cook until it forms a firm ball in cold water (240°F), stirring constantly to prevent sticking. Add vanilla and pour into buttered pans. When cold remove from pan and lay on an oiled bread board. With a long sharp knife and using a saw-like motion cut into inch cubes. Wrap each piece in waxed paper.

PENOCHE

2 cups brown sugar
1 cup white sugar
½ cup Carnation Milk
½ cup water
2 tbsp. corn syrup (light)
2 tbsp. butter
1 tsp. vanilla
½ cup chopped nuts

Mix sugar, corn syrup, and Carnation diluted with the water. Cook until it forms a soft ball in cold water or reaches a temperature of 235°F, stirring occasionally to prevent sticking. Remove from fire, add butter, and let stand until cool. When cool add vanilla and beat until creamy; add chopped nuts and mold on a buttered plate.

OPERA CARAMELS

2 cups sugar

⅓ cup water
⅓ cup Carnation Milk
2 tbsp. corn syrup (light)
2 tbsp. butter
1 tsp. vanilla

Use same method as for Penoche.

½ cup candied cherries (cut in pieces), ½ cup chopped nuts, ½ cup chopped dates, or ½ cup chopped figs may be added just before the candy is molded. After the candy is cut into squares it may be dipped in melted chocolate.

PRALINES

2 cups powdered sugar
1 cup maple syrup
½ cup Carnation Milk
1 cup chopped nuts

Boil sugar, syrup, and Carnation until the mixture forms a soft ball in cold water. Remove from fire, when cool beat until creamy, add nuts and drop from the tip of a spoon in small pieces on a buttered plate. Or the mixture may be molded on a buttered plate and cut into squares.

COCOANUT CREAM CANDY

2 cups sugar
¼ tsp. cream of tartar
1 tbsp. butter
⅓ cup of Carnation Milk
⅓ cup water
½ tsp. vanilla
1 cup shredded cocoanut

Mix sugar, cream of tartar, and Carnation diluted with the water; cook to the soft ball stage. Remove from fire and add butter. When cool add vanilla and beat until creamy. Add cocoanut and drop from spoon into small balls on a buttered plate, or mold on a buttered plate and mark into squares.

Miscellaneous

Among the following miscellaneous recipes you will find several excellent luncheon or supper dishes. The delicious griddle cakes and waffles will be a treat for any meal.

WELSH RAREBIT

2 tbsp. butter
2 tbsp. flour
½ tsp. salt
¼ tsp. mustard
Few grains cayenne
½ cup Carnation Milk
½ cup water
1 egg
½ lb. American cheese

Make a white sauce of the butter, flour, seasonings, and Carnation diluted with water. Add finely cut or grated cheese and stir until melted. Pour hot sauce on beaten egg and mix well. Serve hot on toast. Serves 4.

CARNATION SANDWICH FILLING

1 cup Carnation Milk
½ pound American Cheese (Best to use a package cheese wrapped in tin foil.)
½ can pimiento (small size)
Salt and paprika

Cut cheese in small pieces and add to milk in a double boiler. Heat until the cheese is melted and the mixture is creamy. Remove from the fire immediately, add chopped pimientos, salt, and paprika. This makes a very tasty sandwich spread; it is also delicious served on toast or crackers or used in salads. Keep in a cool place; if too thick when wanted, add more milk and stir well. Makes about 1 pint.

BAKED EGGS A LA CARNATION

1½ tbsp. butter
1½ tbsp. flour
½ tsp. salt
¼ tsp. pepper
½ cup Carnation Milk
½ cup water
4 to 6 eggs
Buttered bread crumbs

Make a white sauce of the butter, flour, seasonings, and Carnation diluted with the water. Pour into a shallow baking dish. Cover the sauce with the eggs, being careful not to break the yolks. Sprinkle buttered bread crumbs over the top and bake in a moderately slow (325°F) oven until eggs are firm. Garnish with parsley.

CARNATION MAKES BETTER BREAD

YEAST BREAD

2 tbsp. shortening
2 tbsp. sugar
2½ tsp. salt
1 cup boiling water
1 cake compressed yeast dissolved in ¼ cup lukewarm water
⅓ cup Carnation Milk
⅔ cup water
7½ cups bread flour, approximately

Put fat, sugar, and salt in a large bowl and pour over it the boiling water and Carnation diluted with ⅔ cup water. When lukewarm (98°F) add the dissolved yeast and 7 cups of flour; stir until thoroughly mixed. Turn dough on to a slightly floured board, knead 10 minutes or until smooth and elastic, adding flour as needed. Put into a bowl, cover and let rise in a warm place (85°F) until double in bulk. Knead dough in the bowl for one minute and again let rise until double in bulk. Cut in half and shape into smooth loaves; place them in a greased pan to again rise until double in bulk. Moisten top with diluted Carnation and place in a hot oven (425°F). Bake about 35 minutes. Makes 2 loaves.

CLOVER LEAF ROLLS

3 tbsp. butter, melted
1 yeast cake dissolved in ¼ cup lukewarm water
⅔ cup Carnation Milk
7½ cups bread flour, approximately
2 tbsp. sugar
2 tsp. salt
1⅓ cups hot water

Add melted butter, sugar, and salt to hot water and Carnation. When lukewarm add the dissolved yeast and mix thoroughly; add flour until dough is stiff enough to knead. Knead for 10 minutes or until dough is smooth and elastic. Let rise in a warm (85°F) place for about 2 hours—until the dough recedes when the hand is thrust into it. Knead dough in the bowl for one minute and again let rise for about 20 minutes. Take small bits of dough, shape into tiny balls and place 3 balls into each greased section of a muffin tin. Let rise until bulk has doubled—about 45 minutes. Bake in a hot (425°F) oven.

CINNAMON ROLLS

Use same dough as for Clover Leaf Rolls. When it is ready to be put in tins roll it to ½ inch thickness, brush with melted butter, sprinkle with a mixture of ½ tbsp. cinnamon, ¼ cup sugar and ½ cup raisins. Roll as a jelly roll. Cut in ¾ inch slices and put into a greased pan. Let rise until the size is doubled. Bake in a hot (425°F) oven for about 20 minutes.

GRIDDLE CAKES

2¼ cups flour
¼ cup cornmeal

4 tsp. baking powder
¼ cup sugar
1 egg, well beaten
⅔ cup Carnation Milk
1⅓ cups water
4 tbsp. fat (melted)
1 tsp. salt

Sift the dry ingredients; dilute the Carnation with the water; add beaten egg to the milk and melted fat. Stir liquid quickly into the dry ingredients. Pour or dip batter out carefully on the hot lightly greased griddle. When the cakes are puffed, full of bubbles, and brown on the edges turn and cook the other side. The griddle should be hot enough so that a cake will brown on one side in 2 minutes.

CARNATION DISHES ARE DELICIOUS

WAFFLES

1½ cups pastry flour
½ tsp. salt
3 tsp. baking powder
2 eggs
⅓ cup Carnation Milk
⅔ cup water
1 tbsp. butter (melted)
1 tbsp. sugar

Sift the dry ingredients. Dilute the Carnation with the water. Beat eggs until foamy, add milk and melted fat. Stir liquids quickly into dry ingredients. Bake in a hot waffle iron until brown and crisp.

DOUGHNUTS

1½ tbsp. butter
⅔ cup sugar

2 eggs
5 tsp. baking powder
¾ tsp. salt
3 tbsp. Carnation Milk
6 tbsp. water
¼ tsp. nutmeg
4 cups bread flour
½ tsp. cinnamon

Cream butter and sugar, add beaten eggs and beat until light and fluffy. Dilute the Carnation with the water. Sift dry ingredients and add them with the milk, combining quickly; toss on a slightly floured board—pat or roll out to ⅓ inch thickness. Cut with a doughnut cutter. Fry in deep hot fat (365°F)—hot enough to brown a one inch cube of bread in 60 seconds. About 2 minutes is required for cooking. Drain on soft paper and roll in confectioner's sugar.

CORN CHOWDER

1½ inch cube of fat salt pork
1 small onion, diced
2 tbsp. butter
2 tbsp. flour
4 cups raw potatoes, diced
2 cups Carnation Milk
2 cups water
⅛ tsp. pepper
8 crackers
1 No. 2 can corn
1½ tsp. salt

Cut pork into small pieces and fry out the fat; add onion and cook until brown. Strain fat into a sauce pan, add potatoes cut in ½ inch cubes, 2 cups of boiling water, and 1 tsp. salt; simmer until tender. Then add the white sauce made of the butter, flour, seasonings, and Carnation diluted with the water. Add the corn and heat the mixture to the boiling point. Place a cracker in a soup plate, dish chowder and serve immediately. Serves 10.

CLAM CHOWDER

¾ inch cube of fat salt pork
½ small onion, diced
2 tbsp. butter
2 cups raw potatoes, diced
2 tbsp. flour
1 tsp. salt
¼ tsp. pepper
1 can minced clams (7 oz. can)
1 cup Carnation Milk
1 cup water

Cut pork into small pieces and fry out the fat; add onion and cook until brown. Strain fat into a sauce pan, add potatoes cut in ½ inch cubes, 1 cup of boiling water, and 1 tsp. salt; simmer until tender. Then add the white sauce made of the butter, flour, seasonings, and Carnation diluted with the water. Add the minced clams with their liquor and heat to the boiling point. Place a cracker in a soup plate, dish chowder and serve immediately. Serves 5.

WHIPPED CARNATION MILK

1 cup Carnation Milk
¼ tsp. gelatine

Soak the gelatine in a tablespoon of cold Carnation; dissolve this in the remaining milk which should be at the boiling point. Cool by placing in a bowl surrounded by cracked ice. When cold whip until stiff. Sweeten and flavor to taste.

CARNATION FOR HOT AND COLD BEVERAGES

Beverages

Coffee creamed with Carnation has a rich color and delightful flavor. Carnation gives to cocoa that delicious creaminess and richness so much desired and adds to its food value.

COCOA

    3 tbsp. cocoa (For children 2 tbsp. cocoa)
    2 tbsp. sugar
    ½ cup hot water
    1½ cups Carnation Milk
    1½ cups water
    ¼ tsp. vanilla
    Few grains salt

Mix cocoa, sugar, and salt and add the hot water; cook over a low fire about 10 minutes. Add the Carnation which has been scalded with the water; cook mixture in a double boiler for 10 minutes; add the vanilla. Whisk with a Dover egg beater just before serving. Place a marshmallow in the cup and pour over it the hot cocoa.

CHOCOLATE

    2 cups Carnation Milk
    2 cups water
    ⅓ cup sugar
    Few grains salt
    2 squares bitter chocolate
    ½ cup water

Scald the Carnation and water and add to it the sugar and salt. Shave chocolate fine; add the ½ cup of water and heat over a low fire until smooth. Combine chocolate mixture and scalded milk. Continue cooking in a double boiler for 10 minutes. Serves 5.

COFFEE

½ cup coffee, ground medium
½ egg
½ cup cold water
3 cups boiling water
¼ cup cold water

Mix the egg and ½ cup cold water and add to the coffee in the pot. Add boiling water, boil up once, stir with a spoon and boil up again. Add the ¼ cup cold water to settle coffee. Serve immediately. Cream with undiluted Carnation. Serves 5.

EGG NOG

1 egg
Few grains salt
2 tbsp. fruit juice
1 tbsp. sugar
⅔ cup ice cold Carnation Milk
⅔ cup ice cold water
Few gratings of nutmeg

Add salt to egg white and beat until stiff. Beat yolk until thick and lemon colored; add the fruit juice and sugar. Dilute Carnation with the water and combine with yolk mixture. Pour into a tall glass, add nutmeg gratings and put egg white on top. Sprinkle top with chopped nuts and serve at once. Serves 2.

CHOCOLATE MALTED MILK

1½ tbsp. malted milk
1½ tsp. cocoa
1 tsp. sugar
Few grains salt
½ cup water
½ cup Carnation Milk
Few drops of vanilla

Mix the malted milk powder, cocoa, sugar, salt, and water, stirring well. Cook for 3 minutes. Add Carnation and vanilla. Serve very hot or ice cold. Makes 1 glass of malted milk.

www.ingramcontent.com/pod-product-compliance
Lightning Source LLC
Chambersburg PA
CBHW080022110526
44587CB00021BA/3742